Unfuckable Lardass

Also by Catriona Strang

Busted (with Nancy Shaw)

*Corked**

Light Sweet Crude (with Nancy Shaw)

Low Fancy

*Reveries of a Solitary Biker**

As editor

*The Gorge: Selected Writing of Nancy Shaw**

* Published by Talonbooks

Unfuckable Lardass

Poems

Catriona Strang

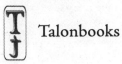

Talonbooks

Talonbooks
9259 Shaughnessy Street, Vancouver, British Columbia, Canada v6p 6r4
talonbooks.com

Talonbooks is located on xʷməθkʷəy̓əm, Sḵwx̱wú7mesh, and səl̓ilwətaʔɬ Lands.

First printing: 2022

Typeset in Jenson
Printed and bound in Canada on 100% post-consumer recycled paper

Interior design by Typesmith
Cover design by andrea bennett with Typesmith
Cover image by andrea bennett

Talonbooks acknowledges the financial support of the Canada Council for the Arts, the Government of Canada through the Canada Book Fund, and the Province of British Columbia through the British Columbia Arts Council and the Book Publishing Tax Credit.

Library and Archives Canada Cataloguing in Publication

Title: Unfuckable lardass : poems / Catriona Strang.
Names: Strang, Catriona, author.
Identifiers: Canadiana 20210278277 | isbn 9781772013887 (softcover)
Classification: lcc ps8587.t679 u54 2022 | ddc c811/.54—dc23

for my mother
Alison Strang, 1931–2018

and for my children
Nina Houle and Felix Houle

Oceans of Love

Summer Sampler

at times I do
regain equilibrium
enough to refute

rebukes enough
to claim me

unfuckable lardass
to claim
you, I
refuse

Cleft or rift, Hellebore and Oxalis, gone

before she left. Not quite hardy under average

Unfuckable
Lardass

---

contrasting finely. With threadlike creeping

What's with the hair?

You some kinda rebel?

—U.S. BORDER GUARD, 2018

---

stems, I had a habit of coming up against her

I.

Bitch-burn's lunged here
a long time
(borne quite
a tale)
with hail-makers and
others' dread
unravelling

how we revelled, we read of
refusal's emergence, of
        what else
                would you have?
bearing unbending (*I can't*
fucking bear it), of
unborne or illicit
unburdened but
performed (*I won't*
fucking do it)
refuse perforated by unstable
elusives burning not
to burn

it's been a long
fucking time

better judgment. Finely peppered with a mist of

2.

of loquacity's mumbling and
tended flowers quenching
burning wood, of
the quilty grips of viscous,
funky, splintering sips
who'd go piling against gain
and nubbing and looping
and flowing against again
and again again
and

dark red, it's time to dig in deeply. Sometimes

3. Let Us Recapitulate

to make hands
useless, disorder
minds, strike
at the act of re
production, poison
flowers, break
arms, make
hail and miss
carriage, attack
the marriage bed
(it's said)

lands covered
with grapes and corn

candles blown
out despite
the setting sun

wheat, hay, manure, rain, snow
storms, heretics, lepers

entirely too kindly. But by fire of patience folded

feet
firmly
planted

waffles and cracknels
baskets, bottles of lemonade

all never
quite brought
to heel

together at their first coming forth, I may yet

4.

said it
all
before

decide to run rampant. You're either aggressive

5.

implied concealment.
spikes a handy spit
(we can't handle
the sporting sense)

here clasping cloaks
or manacles our
handy, under
handed spirit

and weaves our
mighty slyness

or weedy, a spreader for a choice spot.   *My*

6. Aubergine

for Ted Byrne

oh, burgeon
ill burden
whose glossy
loft buds
burnished, swells
beamish: I'll bite
unbidden

roots remain thready; I love a purple sheen on

7. Yell, Danielle

for Danielle LaFrance

I'm whatever
the sea throws up

we're salted wreck
and who *could*

sing under such
conditions? Tongues

taught to stammer
and swallow slip

avid on
supplanted

ply, pry the
civil tongue right

out of my
head: here's

stones, kestrels
a gale-force wrack

the underside. Occasionally I still weep for her.

8.

my unmeasured response
melts paltry, flips
rogue quivers or tears
seizures (now that
decades have ripped on by)

beets, pumpkins, cabbage
honey, milk, everything
in pots

now repose fuses improbable
impossible impossible
ever to forget her raspy
ragged gasps and
her ceasing

But before slight variations have taken effect, I

9. Handy

for Mum

pressing pastry into
pie plates suddenly
bums, noses, hands, faces,
teary eyes, bleeding
bodies, coldy chests, all
wiped, stomachs rubbed, diapers
changed, shit, pee, vomit, pus,
snot, spills, excreta
of all kinds re
contained, books held, pages
turned, teeth
brushed, bodies
washed, creams and lotions
smeared, medicines
administered, spots
scrubbed, slivers
extracted, band-aids
applied, babies
carried, cradled, caressed,
hair washed, brushed,
cut, braided – heads
whacked hard – sheets
stripped and replaced, mops,

— — — — — — — — — — — — — — — —

run the gamut. We fall too quickly (oh to rise

brooms, vacuums, prams,
strollers pushed, clothes
made and mended, curtains
sewn, sheets
repaired, hats, mitts,
scarves and sweaters knit, hugs
given, jugs and bottles
filled and emptied, astonishing,
food shared, bikes pushed and
carried, plates and cutlery laid
and cleared, dishes
washed, put away, taken
out, animals, flowers,
sunlight pointed
out, cards, notes, letters
written, forms signed,
precarity steadied, hot
water bottles filled,
presents wrapped and
unwrapped, poultices
administered, laundry scrubbed,
put into machines and
lifted out again, hung
up and taken down, folded, put

---

early, and with vigour), ever indispensable in the

away, clothes put on
and taken off, ice packs
applied, foreheads
wiped, compost and
garbage disposed
of, groceries selected,
carried, unpacked,
stored, taken out, holes
dug and filled, seeds
planted, spoons offered, dead
pets buried, apples, cherries,
rhubarb, raspberries, peas,
beans, potatoes, lettuce picked
and washed, tea steeped,
my cold hands hers,
lunches packed, drinks
steadied, jams, jellies,
pickles and chutneys
simmered, chopping,
stirring, mixing, baking,
roasting, frying, burning,
serving, eating
accomplished, pastry
rolled and shaped,

smallest garden. Struggling in the intricate folds

canes and walkers
held and not
held, glasses found and
lost, pies, tarts, muffins,
cakes, cookies, scones baked
shoes tied and
untied, age spots
emerging, skin
crêping, flowers
gathered in

of my own implications, relationships are rarely

10.

Men have broad shoulders and narrow
hips and accordingly possess intelligence.
—MARTIN LUTHER

unwieldy, weary
wary, the long west
immolates us
all, summary
lurching repository of
disjointing social
functions it does not
represent, or embolden
or embroaden any
welched way

obvious.   I harbour regret. Bells at the first

II.

lent lift rarely —
flowers, samplers, stump
work — we witness
constraints and contra
dictions, every conceivable
surface a community
memory, the same
wretched harangue the
vanguard in a
time of vultures

suspicion of milder air — who would not dwindle,

12. The Amalgam

I am contending factions. Even in times of great
dispute and intense social trauma, an amalgam
of functions does not represent. Some days
are prose. Can a visual record be a vehicle of
community? Considering the efficacy of barley
soup (it is conceivable that I have succumbed to
the latent ideology of *The Modern Cook's Year*),
I become over-mapped. It's *my* tradition to pick
it till it bleeds.

on the cusp of weaker growth? They have also a

13.

discussion or incursion
invention or diversion

it was all good until I
rolled over and flattened it

any wonder
we were born
rebellious and enraged?

at this rate
I'll be itching
for days

certain cleansing faculty. Now come the aches

Niceness vs. the performance of niceness: stop
and observe the ceaseless intersections of shifting
social clusters. How is this possible? Tracing her
fractured mind, we are none of us individuals –
now when can I get back to aimless net surfing?
I'm constitutionally obedient *and* rebellious, a
wobbly accumulation of labour and error, and yes
I'm still bleeding. It's not *maybe*, it's your *inhaler*.

and pains of the muscles and joints, the sunburn,

15.

new green shoots again
welcome wonder's
edge rippling
torn up replete
rates joyous ply
now baffle-cavorting
uphill and down

the strains of the quotidian. For fuck's sake help

16.

Quickly, its head
wide, an alley, a
house – we're
familiar. By the
afternoon, failure.

keep it alive. I've never been entirely hardy,

17.

Sometimes, like the camel, I could just spit.

in the ordinary sense. In the darkest night they

18.

I objected to his scale of values.
—SIMONE DE BEAUVOIR

Expanding every
always. Grief
born of inter
minable struggles
with an intrusive
fact, washed
with green.

Define "public."
Now define
"interest."

I bear it. I saw
night inventing
you, burgeon
burly; I have
eaten every
thing.

— — — — — — — — — — — — — — — — —

need no description. Fretting, eating, swelling, or

19.

Grip-steamed by
placating post
asshole im
plications, slammed

or trimmed
by grief, tears
assault me

all rips and no
slip-gap, no
map

corroding, we will all scab and itch. By reason of

20.

watching
emerged
before

a so-called public
whose long-oiled
forgetting

some storied youth
that was not
my mother, gone

yesterday, this

banality for
nothing, "come
look, but come ..."

to a beginning
in an over
looking

— — — — — — — — — — — — — — — —

great weight entering into the skin, an immense

I might
comfort history
a con

dition of
living
you then bring

or brink the
unblinking story stood
up, borrowed

as heroic fire night
hawks failed to
fill, night

fall holding

relief to the overworked. Mother, be effectual.

21. Daffodils for the Dying

I can
not love
old corrupt
toadies of
an envious
petrified
insane
arc, sun
and moon
same sky

above, crows
bathe: we've
our handy might
all sly
in one
sky

A soft and safe medicine for days of shade — in

22.

don't

with me

compost provided with rich ingredients, who

23.

flavour fervour
will winch
an arch
or inch

defence: just
don't funk it
dearie

knows who may be expelled?   How often I

24.

Deleterious lessons unlearned – I'll write no more
of this lifetime's unravelling. It drove me out of all
measure, and all I did was scrawl a fucking poem,
though I sang my mother across. I will not now
undertake to say, as some do, that equilibrium can
never be attained. But whose "normal" do we refer
to? And how are you?

confuse myself. Still she's not here. Perhaps I

25. the aftermath: a list of difficulties

with birdsong, morning
becomes electric, relentless
sea muck overseen
tidal and under
bred, unsigned
unmourned, maybe
even morbid

might carry away on the wind – despite hoary

26.

One Thursday night I notice the uniqueness of
each body in the Killarney pool change room,
although none of them bear the sleek, smoothed,
subtly primped sheen only regular infusions of time
and capital can bestow, and though annie said I
should write about the tenacity of the wildlife on
the river beneath the Oak Street Bridge — wrens,
kinglets, sparrows, hummingbirds, herring, bees,
seals, blackberries, tansy, fennel, willow, alder,
mushrooms, oak — how they seem to thrive right
in the midst of tugboats, tractors, cranes, barges,
logjams, cement plants, cars, trucks, bridges, trains,
airplanes, garbage — capital's relentless onslaught —
tonight swimming in this crowded pool all I can
think about is how the streetlight reflected off the
dark, rain-slicked pavement, shifting and glittering
like sunlight on the sea, reminds me of the many
nights my young body spent tramping through the
streets in the wet dark, circulating through the city
like streams of shining water filled with a plethora
of body types, like ducks bobbing on the river.

remembrances of inconstancy and sudden mutability,

27.

Of fetid fistulae
enrobed, awaiting
and not
pretensing

as if control
were not illusory

or intentions
never misread

as if love
misremembered

or tensions
finite

which come from beyond the sea, my comrades

28.

for Fred Wah

The stop not a trick. When fixity gives the
appearance of inscription, think again. To beat
the feeling heart, imperfectly, is probably the best
we can pop for. To review, to survive, and not to
foresee. (Here it is again, the illusion of tracing
thought through time, a webbing woven from
within.) Yet again, my intentions have changed.

and I continue swimming toward the moon.   It's a

29. "The Ravelled Sleeve of Care"

a day of very little
but every containment grief-stunned

or slammed with burst conceivability
an intimate familiarity

don't give me
any fucking grief

could be my boundaries
blur, but I'd say the

politics of my appearance
remain self-explanatory

— — — — — — — — — — — — —

long, slow bolt. Like cats in a bucket, we very

much delight in tumbling and wallowing. Now

So that's the bottomless
depths of my love divided
by the number of times
I inadvertently take
a screenshot trying to
turn off my phone.

---

what breeds peppery in the belly? We'll never be

By Patient Accumulation Also

rid of that familiar gnawing of the heart, though

Capitalism is the latest
avatar of patriarchy.

—MARIA MIES

— — — — — — — — — — — — — — — —

it can feel comfortable for the head and memory.

begin one sway
my ease beguiles none
whose wiles beg also
"be ever-sallied," this way
the river dews all, so
here is tacit, hey?

To those as have stirred up venery: I never said

picking myself apart
rapts all part's lift
and flicks curious reflection;
let's slough off all
peaks, my peaks
give flex to too many
scurrilous scrapings
to reach this
sure reef's shore

I didn't harbour regret.   As could happen

whose lustre cracks
a basket's charm
to flaunt and lull or
lope these fluted slopes

almost anywhere in an open situation. There's a

to lease
myself to pieces
too loose to attend
I was laced
closely pierced
of myself
embroiled to
pieces, I was attended
too closely, I was
wasted, unattended
my body in pieces
embroidered no peace

yellow thrum about you, nicked about the edges.

to truncate closely
attends conical, or spills

cones, tends hills
to trundle loosely

to implicate slowly
shills the torn end

tin hills limp sore
not tonned, or shrill

it'll rend my tone
asunder, this thin heap

placates sundry
round, old tory

dunce, this sun's
ply will dry

your tune: we've
done so

Perhaps we now suffer from siege melancholy;

but in the grandeur of
all our parts
we know differently
whose anti
recusals could not
be exceeded

let's succour our sisters, women. For all the good

bloody clouts and gobs

— — — — — — — — — — — — — —

she provides, the taste can be very bitter. Often

before boundaries
bear my breaks
I'll slip common symptoms
sideways, or sip
no comfort, not
unless nothing
spikes between
rot's froth

there's a swimming and turning, a desire I cannot

identify. Because though I love to grow among

I do what I'm knowing

subtracted from I have no

idea where I put my keys.

— — — — — — — — — — — — — —

rubbish, I do get pains in my head.   Step softly;

This
Rabble
World

I am reddened and enflamed. Ours is a vicious

I want all these things
to stay with you,
let nothing remain
in this rabble world
in this forsaken year,
that once made us
think it was beautiful.

—BERTAN DE BORN
translated by
FREDERICK GOLDIN

— — — — — — — — — — — —

culture. Although practising social isolation, I

I.

getting cozy
with uncertainty

there's a bee
full of cherries

remain aggrieved; after all, there are pains a

2.

moon
humming
woodsy

sugared violet cannot diminish – oh for a fine,

3.

just about
pop-ready

that's got
my what

tart relish to throb against ease. But this is ever

4.

impending absolute
blossom riot

our charge. And the thing spoiled. No mitigating

5.

trees
wind
ing

this, as a
posit
ion, shuns

factors, other than the teeth to eat them gleaming

6.

this dying
thing is
killing me

in a rich man's mouth. I may roarip, but let us

7.

who's ever
got a lock
on it

not mistake the brain for the nose. Please step

8.

so divert
me, sure

back, in consideration of my narcissist allergy.

9.

sipping frozen
here as
buds unfurl

And now the distinct and pungent dreams of

10.

lingering lilac
the airy rain

old women grow wild; what could be more

II.

to decide:
the rose, the
lupin, the lily
of the valley

the tenacity of
the beach
pea

fitting and gloriously thorny, now that love has

12.

witness the un
ravelling

corroded all the way down to disgust? I assert

13.

whose voice
of biting
experience?

nothing, despite remaining snippy about the

That'll be the number
of clothes pegs dropped
and lost in plain sight
multiplied by how many
times a night one person
can possibly get up to pee.

— — — — — — — — — — — — — — — — —

edges. It would appear I like mine selfish, but

Lake
Lac

for John Dowland

---

what of my ribs?   *Because word problems*

*Nature shrinks as
capital grows.*

—VANDANA SHIVA

- - - - - - - - - - - - - - - - -

appear harder. How often I fall for my own

I.

I lack the capacity adequately to theorize the extent
of my own lackings. We may lack. I might be a
lackey. Consider the ways in which we currently
lack. I lament my lackings, they drive me to tears,
but I try not to swim in Lake Lac. Sometimes I
admit my lacks with alacrity. On good days, I can
manage my lackings. There's acrimony in my lacks.
Lack we may.

tricks, rambling over any suitable support. It turns

2.

Old Tears:
Like a lit match.

Tears of Relief:
Renew anew.

Tears of Disbelief:
After the drenching I took.

Tears of Rage:
There's giddiness and simmering in my head.

Tears of Despair:
How often I confuse myself.

Enraptured Tears:
Be a mother. Lose a mother.

Joyful Tears:
"We are not alone in this process."

Tears of Exhaustion:
Regret is a long day.

_ _ _ _ _ _ _ _ _ _ _ _ _ _ _ _

out brittleness in the stem does not suit ordinary

Crisis Tears:
Chilblains as cultural heritage.

Mother's Tears:
Wave the yellow flag of transition.

Worker's Tears:
Against the gnawing of the heart.

Concussed Tears:
Now *here's* a list of difficulties.

Evening Tears:
Consider the architecture of emotion.

Overwrought Tears:
O my inconstant hormones.

Lover's Tears:
So often I just need to go home.

Tears of Pain:
But calculate the anxieties projected
onto our grandmothers' bodies.

purposes, even in those as do love strong savours.

Invisible Tears:
Become performative.

Excessive Tears:
Cats are very much delighted.

Performative Tears:
Many hurt more.

Breakdown Tears:
Slot me in.

Collective Tears:
Ribbed right through.

Exultant Tears:
Wherein I reveal no body shape.

— — — — — — — — — — — — — — — —

There's a piercing quality to the griefs in my

3. Big Salty Mama

here's how refusal's
bearing elucidates
a flipping
or stepping
in, yeah I'll
take it, carriage

and candle as
redone plunder
implanted then
ripped out

an implied burden
assumed ragged
as when Merkel
fucking carried on

not remnants but restitution

and doesn't function represent?
ceaseless labour inhaled
and consumed

head, not eased by spikes or promises of a caring

maybe salt's tang
underwrites maybe
grief implodes maybe
assholes slip maybe
the public is
banal maybe I'm
failing maybe this
is a flavour, sure

deleterious defence
has never not
been tricky

future. These need no description, and not only

4.

I grew it
I tended
it I harvested
dried and
stored it
I knocked
it over and
smashed
it

because my interest has already wandered – here

The lengths I wouldn't
go for you to the power
of the number of nouns
I lose per day.

------- — -- — — — -- — — — -- — — --

I may have to assert my right to be a pain in

Fuck
Variations

----

the ass (now there's a pattern worth breaking).

At some point the social

fabric will be all stains.

—COLIN SMITH

——— —— —— —— —— —— —— —— ——

It's my bad-bad, which will have to serve as

unjustly fuck-belly
rupture, hopeless
insert or rough chat
counsel – some lens
for unseeing all we
did fuck
up

an answer, because word problems sound

sometimes pain fucks
me sideways, Anglo
Saxon straining at
my own margins my
wracked back sets
my teeth in the
mouth-margin
sometimes I can't stand
grit-fucking, sometimes
that's my fretful de
centred edge

easier. *Imagine a means of assessment other*

banned, or rather
braying of
some fertile's

joy or sad
misfortune, this
doing's not

delight
though need's
not caught

in expectation's
diversion, in
hope and agony

in hair and eyes all
necked, fuck
this, I was

nicked, all this time
there's been naked
forces brewing

than sexual use value. To refute, to refuse, to

there's still hard
grit between
my teeth

*and what about
the debt-fucked?*

fulling buds on my
feckless brain, but
loan me any other
fucking function

flip. Who can say they are not currently in a

A woman with a cudgel changes tense in order to be seen. Plough the fucking fields, and what would I be fit for? Despite the relief in loss, I became a subject merely due to my associations. Fuck it! – "Now we see the violence inherent in the system." Ruin, spoil, exhaust, or wear out [insert hapless intensifier here]. "We don't care what you say," and no, I don't care to mess around.

tangled state? Let's go creeping wild; I'm a tender

when did I
come so closely
to resemble
the Venus of
Willendorf how
deep into the
earth might my
spine dissolve why
am I ambivalent how
hard my tongue can
press against my
teeth how far
will that red stain
spread feels
good until
you stop
scratching how
messed up
is that

plant, but as when Merkel simply carried on,

but will
we adapt?

certain avenues
have never

opened ingestion
brings me

comfort could
a leaf's

architecture constitute
revamped heritage?

I know what I
need I'm

serious here
there's been

a lot
of blood

will inhabit a supposedly undesirable space. Let

despite the systems still
inscribing me, I do get tired
of explaining how to pronounce
my name – whose ribs

get breathing room?
what ripped inscription
infuses possibility? what's
this peeling? now

explain my crabbed
script it's possible I kid
myself but of course there's
still pleasure to be had

me be grown apart. Ours no more a basis for a

sideways straining
in this mouth-grit, some
fulsome folly or
febrile [inset rupture], graft's
candid rustling grips
ruin, all roiling: people, what
the fuck?

— — — — — — — — — — — — — —

system of government than strange women lying

in ponds.   Help the mother in her weariness

Coda: TGFI

---

jasmine there is no mention. Even if it cannot

TGFI

*with andrea bennett, annie ross, Christine Stewart,
Colin Smith, Danielle LaFrance, Felix Houle,
Jacquie Leggatt, Jenny Lee, Karen Fleming, Kiel Strang,
Matea Kulić, Molly Rader, Nina Houle, Shawk Alani,
Talia Strang, and an anonymous contributor. Love and
thanks to them all.*

Lately it's one shitstorm after another for the Girl
    from Ipanema.
The Girl from Ipanema wants no part of your
    fantasies.
A grrl from Compton is tanned from walking to
    the bus stop on the corner of Imperial and
    Paramount.
By the way, our girl is a boy.
Middle-aged men drive up on Some grrl from
    Compton, dirty mouth, rolled-down windows.
The Girl from the Grand Union Hotel never gets old.
The Girl from Ipanema is a mutant centipede.
The Girl from East Van drains a three at the buzzer.
She scores the winning goal.
The Girl from Ipanema stops walking, rips your man
    heart right out of your stupid man ribcage, and
    dances on it.

— — — — — — — — — — — — — — — —

strictly be said, I do maintain that this grief

The Boi from Ipanema wears her bathing suit under
    her shorts.
This Girl from Ipanema has back pain.
Don't fuck with her.
She remains unpaid.
No way does the girl respond to your response to her.
She declines to be Albertine.
A grrl from Compton always looks over her shoulder.
The Girl from Ipanema takes up kickboxing.
The Girl from Broad Street prorogues you.
Compton grrls will mess you up.
While eating a sandwich, the Girl reading Ahmed
    wonders if the singer is sincere.
The Girl from Ipanema says no.
Why does a grrl from Compton stop, turn, give the
    death stare to anyone coming up too close from
    behind?
The Girl from the Grand Union Hotel dreams of
    animus ginch burning.
The Girl from East Van crushes that ball.
The Girl from Ipanema radiates her life force.
Our girl prefers not to.
Imagine why she looks straight ahead.
The girl plans her next meal.

exceeds the stings of wasps and bees. "Neither

And says, "Greetings, comrade, looks like your dick's
    still capitalist, eh?"
The Girl in the Mud Puddle's got songs to do and
    things to sing.
The Girl from Ottawa casts a vote of non-confidence.
For what it's worth, the Girl from the Grand Union
    Hotel thinks Frank Sinatra is Woody Allen's
    favourite conductor.
The Girl from Granada is wrapped up in her thesis.
The Girl from Ipanema can't go on.
The Girl from Trikinetic locates the pain.
Our girl sings her own song.
The Girl from Unceded Musqueam Territory wonders
    if she needs to oil the joint hinge.
She goes for a swim.
And considers her mortality, asshole.
This girl repels legislative attack.
She is not "in control" of her material.
The Girl from Mosul thinks about smoking a cigarette.
The Girl from Granada doesn't make eye contact.
Our girl is beginning to remember.
And says, "Eat my fuck."
Shocker! They may not take up reproductive labours.
The Boi from Ipanema, her thighs are sticky, chafing.

witch nor devil, thunder nor lightning," according

The Girl from Broad Street just wants to ride the
    fucking bus.
Girls will go on.
The Girl reading Ahmed wonders if the Girl from
    Ipanema is related to Guantanamera, the Girl from
    Guantánamo.
The Girl from Ipanema reads Federici.
She is an autonomous subject.
She calls the election.
While considering her reproductive options.
The Girl from Broad Street filibusters.
And repels the gaze.
The Girl from Unceded Musqueam Territory squares
    the circle.
The ocean is what the Girl from Ipanema calls "grand."
The grrl from Compton daydreams of Cinderella's
    fate, fast-food work, mass graves.
She rejects your reality and substitutes virtually
    anyone else's.
The Girl from Prescott resolves the seventh.
The Girl from Unceded Musqueam Territory harvests
    dahlias.
Our girl leaps the moon.
Leave the girl alone.

— —

to Culpeper, and yet itching and scratching

The Girl from Mosul will strangle you, hang you in
   black cloth.
Our girl dreams of a striking snake.
And just keeps going.
The Girl from East Van puts that shit in the trees
   four-seventy.
The bitterness of the failed patriarch is not this
   girl's primary concern.
The Girl from the Car Wash votes you out.
The girl weaves strands of beach grass.
She has her grandmother's sharp tongue.
They walk off their cramps.
They want housing for all.
The Girl from the Grand Union Hotel watches
   the boy so sadly.
The Girl from Trikinetic breathes.
The Girl from Ipanema will never be a farmer.
As luck would have it, the Girl from the Grand
   Union Hotel sleep sways.
Our girl is a frail fucken flower.
She hoes a fine row.
The Girl from Ottawa exits without a deal.
The Girl from Ithaca just wants to work on her
   weaving.

continue. How often I grow impatient; imagine a

Our girl stands her ground.
She produces copious bodily fluids.
And descends to the underworld.
She would kill for a cup of tea.
The Girl from Mosul was here before you.
The Girl from Ipanema isn't from Ipanema.
She says, "Shaka, when the walls fell."
And lactates.
She is not surprised.
The girl mourns her mother.
She spoils her ballot.
And dreads the question-as-performance.
The Girl from Unceded Musqueam Territory
    considers the hypotenuse.
The Girl from Ipanema is a barbaric cultural practice.
She brings it all crashing down.
She lost her hair to chemo.
The girl sports a splendid bush.
The Girl reading Ahmed knows that enough pressure
    buildup can cause a snap, and that "snapping is
    necessary to break a bond," and that the bond is
    the collective tune of patriarchy we hum under
    our breaths.
The Girl from Ipanema has already had all her fun.

healing collective, a raging infection.

She grinds your bones to make her bread.
Some girls are menopausal.
The Girl from Broad Street turns you to stone.
This girl bristles.
Our girl knows humanistic capitalism is an
    oxymoron.
She is not a barometer of public taste.
She has miscarried.
She cultivates a white rose.
And her eyesight is not in question.
The Girl from a place that, alas, is not Narnia is
  · prepared.
Today our girl is a phlegm factory.
The Girl from Ipanema is an unfuckable lardass.
She is a single mum.
Who adorns her hair with seaweed.
And turns a heel before supper.
She is out of the game.
The Girl from the Grand Union Hotel has no interest
    in each ones' feelings but does his. Does his.
The Girl from Ipanema refutes her inner Protestant.
The Girl from Ipanema eats your heart in the
    marketplace.

Of jasmine there remains no mention.

NOTES

This book's title attempts to invert and inhabit
an outrageously sexist insult allegedly levelled at
German Chancellor Angela Merkel in 2011.

Poems 16 and 20 of "Unfuckable Lardass" use
language from George Bowering's *Taking Measures:
Selected Serial Poems*. Other poems in this sequence
are indebted to Emmanuel Le Roy Ladurie's *Jasmin's
Witch* and the writings of Silvia Federici.

"By Patient Accumulation Also" owes much to
Stephen Collis, Charles Darwin, and Karl Marx.

"Lake Lac" was written in response to John
Dowland's *Lacrimae*. The section "Joyful Tears"
quotes Silvia Federici's *Re-Enchanting the World:
Feminism and the Politics of the Commons*.

"Fuck Variations" were written in response to
an invitation from the *Capilano Review*. Thanks
especially to Editorial Director Matea Kulić for the
prompt and the encouragement, and to Inua Ellams's
The Actual for its incendiary example.

"Summer Sampler," the text running at the bottom of the page throughout the book, was inspired by the Bayeux Tapestry and uses language from Maureen and Bridget Boland's *Old Wives' Lore for Gardeners*, Nicholas Culpeper's *Culpeper's Complete Herbal*, Daniel Defoe's *Journal of the Plague Year*, Helena Rutherford Ely's *A Woman's Hardy Garden*, John Gerard's *Gerard's Herbal*, John Halsham's *Every Man's Book of Garden Flowers*, Elizabeth Lawrence's *The Little Bulbs: A Tale of Two Gardens*, Donald Culross Peattie's *Flowering Earth*, Ted Underhill's *Roadside Wildflowers of the Northwest*, and John M. Valleau's *Perennial Gardening Guide*.

The embroidery reproduced on the inside front and back covers was done in Scotland by Eileen Strang, my grandmother, in the early 1940s.

ACKNOWLEDGMENTS

I shared intense distress, worry, grief, stress, disbelief, laughter, and healing with my beloved siblings, Elspeth Strang, Hilary Strang, Al Strang, and Robert Strang, during the declines and deaths of our mother and father, which took place while this book was being written. To them, love and gratitude beyond measure. Love to all the grief-stricken.

Special love and gratitude to Nicole Markotić and Colin Smith for their detailed, perceptive edits. Love, thanks, comradeship, ocean swims, cups of tea, and solidarity also to Matea Kulić, Leah Sharzer, Christine Stewart, Danielle LaFrance, Stephen Collis, Ted Byrne, Alessandra Capperdoni, Louis Cabri, annie ross, Daphne Marlatt, Fenn Stewart, Rhoda Rosenfeld, Teresa Green, Michelle Vega, Jacqueline Leggatt, Kelly Haydon, Felix Houle, Nina Houle, the cousins in science, all my generous collaborators on "TGFI," Renée Sarojini Saklikar for COVID solidarity, and Kim Koch and Rod Clarke of the Paper Hound bookstore.

Thanks to andrea bennett for the wonderful
cover embroidery, to my stalwart and meticulous
colleague Charles Simard, and to everyone else
at Talonbooks – Darren Atwater, Chloë Filson,
Kara Toews, Leslie Smith, Kevin Williams, Spencer
Williams, Vicki Williams, Mocha (RIP), and Rya.

Grateful thanks to the editors of the *Capilano Review*
(Fenn Stewart, Matea Kulić), G U E S T (David
Dowker), *Some* (Robert Manery), and *Tripwire*
(David Buuck), where some of these poems appeared
in earlier forms.

CATRIONA STRANG is the author of *Low Fancy,* *Corked,* and *Reveries of a Solitary Biker,* and co-author of *Busted, Cold Trip,* and *Light Sweet Crude* with the late Nancy Shaw, whose selected works, *The Gorge,* she edited. She frequently collaborates with composer Jacqueline Leggatt, and lives with her two grown kids on unceded xʷməθkʷəy̓əm, Sḵwx̱wú7mesh, and səl̓ilwətaʔɬ Lands.